Seen any apples lately?

Early each year, in orchards and backyards, apple trees bloom.

Drawn by the sweet smell, bees buzz from blossom to blossom.

As time passes, petals flutter to the grass, and fuzzy bumps appear.

Slowly the baby apples grow bigger, turning all shades of red.

A glowing green.
A cheerful yellow.

Apples might have golden speckles or snazzy stripes.

Be round as a ball or tall and lumpy-bottomed.

Limbs droop, heavy with ripe fruit.

Some apples thud to the ground, then rot and become food for the growing tree.

At last it's fall—harvest time!—and fresh apples are everywhere.

Grocery stores. Farmer's markets. Roadside stands.

You might even climb a ladder to pick your own.

Your teeth sink in—crunch!—and tart-sweet juice dribbles down your chin.

People bob for apples at Halloween parties or dip them into melted caramel for a sweet gooey treat.

Apples may be baked into pies and cinnamony desserts or added to a yummy Thanksgiving stuffing.

Some are cooked into thick applesauce or crushed to make juice.

On a chilly night, a steaming mug of tangy cider chases away goosebumps.

Apple trees have been growing in America for hundreds of years— since colonists brought pips, or apple seeds, from England.

When most of America was still unsettled, a pioneer named John Chapman spent his summers hiking through the wilderness, planting apple seeds wherever he went.

His nickname was Johnny Appleseed.

An apple's seeds lie in its core. Cut an apple crosswise and you'll see the shape of a star.

Each of the star pockets has one or two seeds sleeping inside.

Americans eat more apples than any other fruit.

There are many flavors to choose from, with names like Fuji, Gala, Granny Smith, Honeycrisp, Jonathon, McIntosh, Pink Lady, and Red Delicious.

Have *you* found your favorite?

Ahh,
love at first bite!